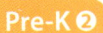

Numbers

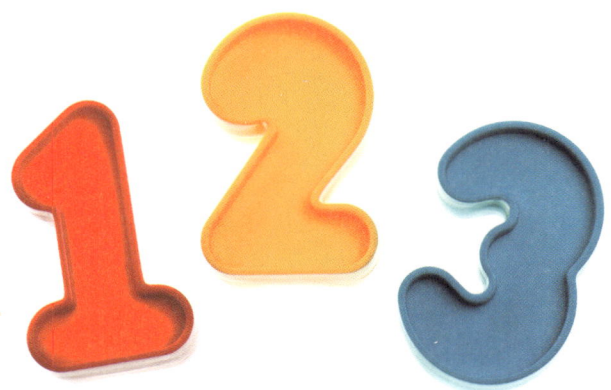

Seed Learning

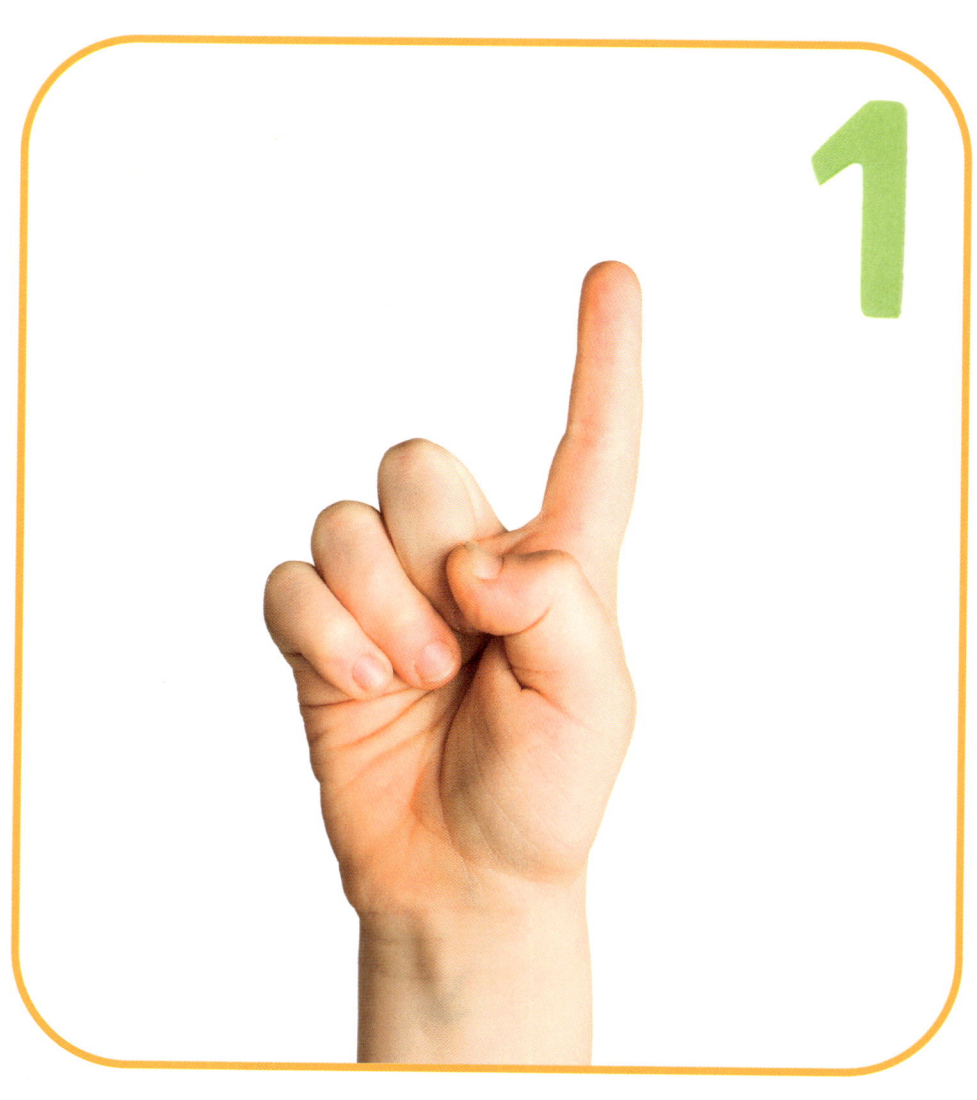

one

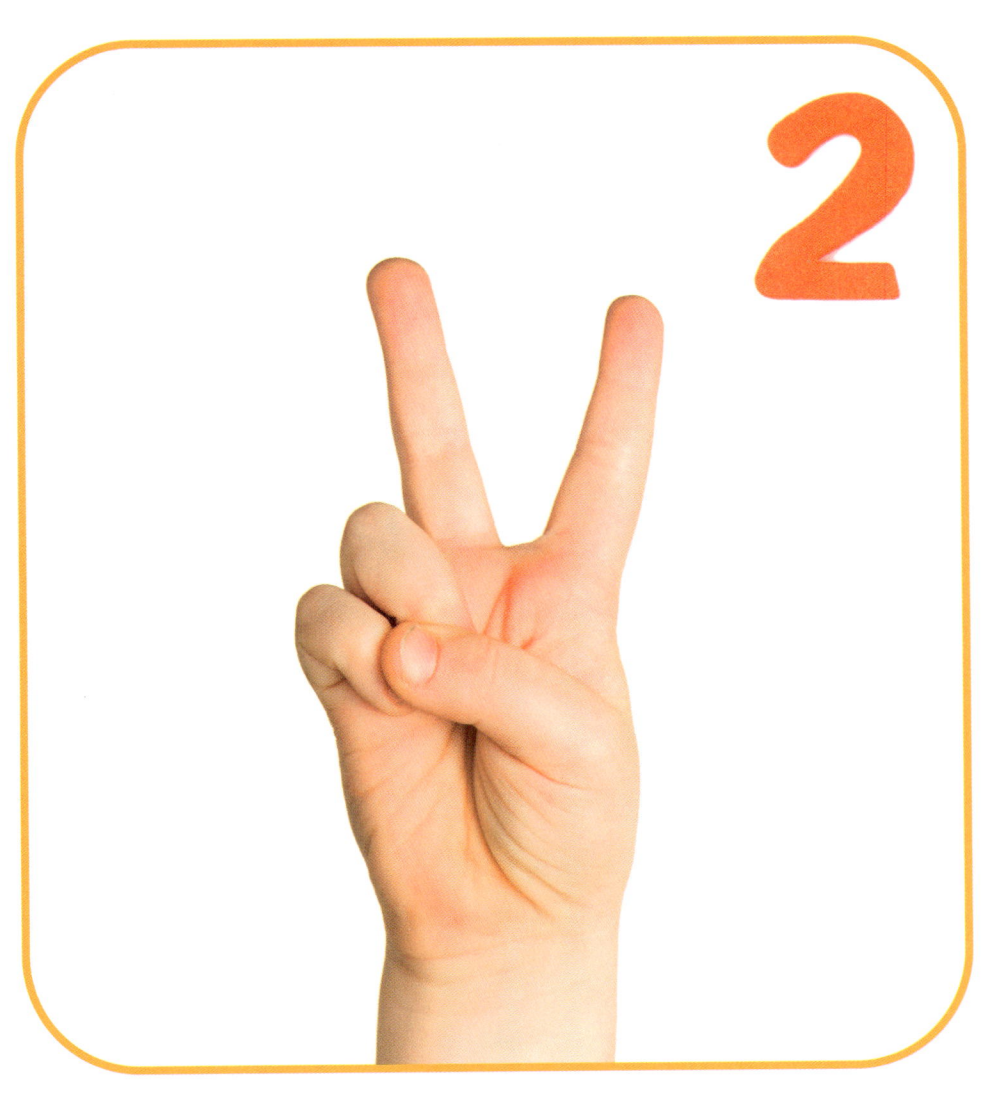

two

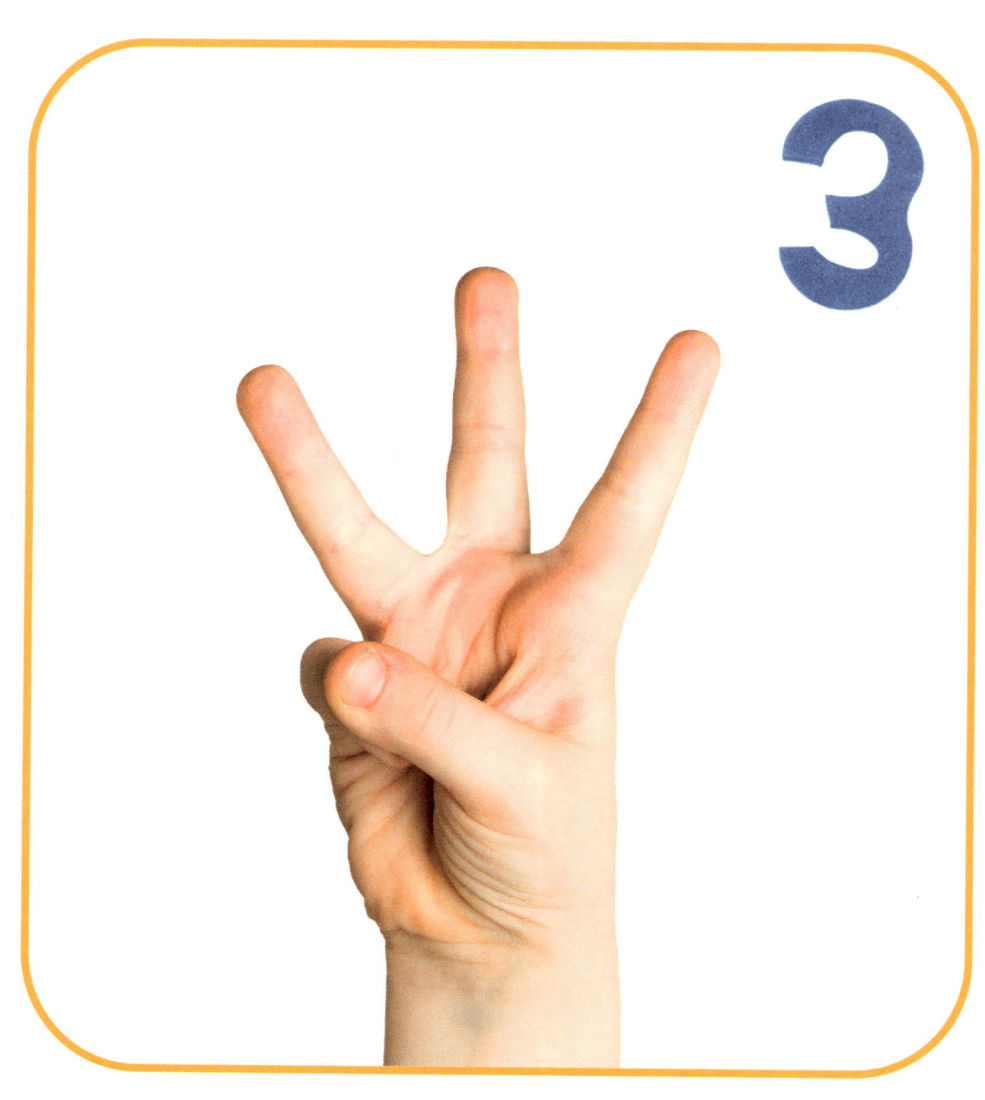

three

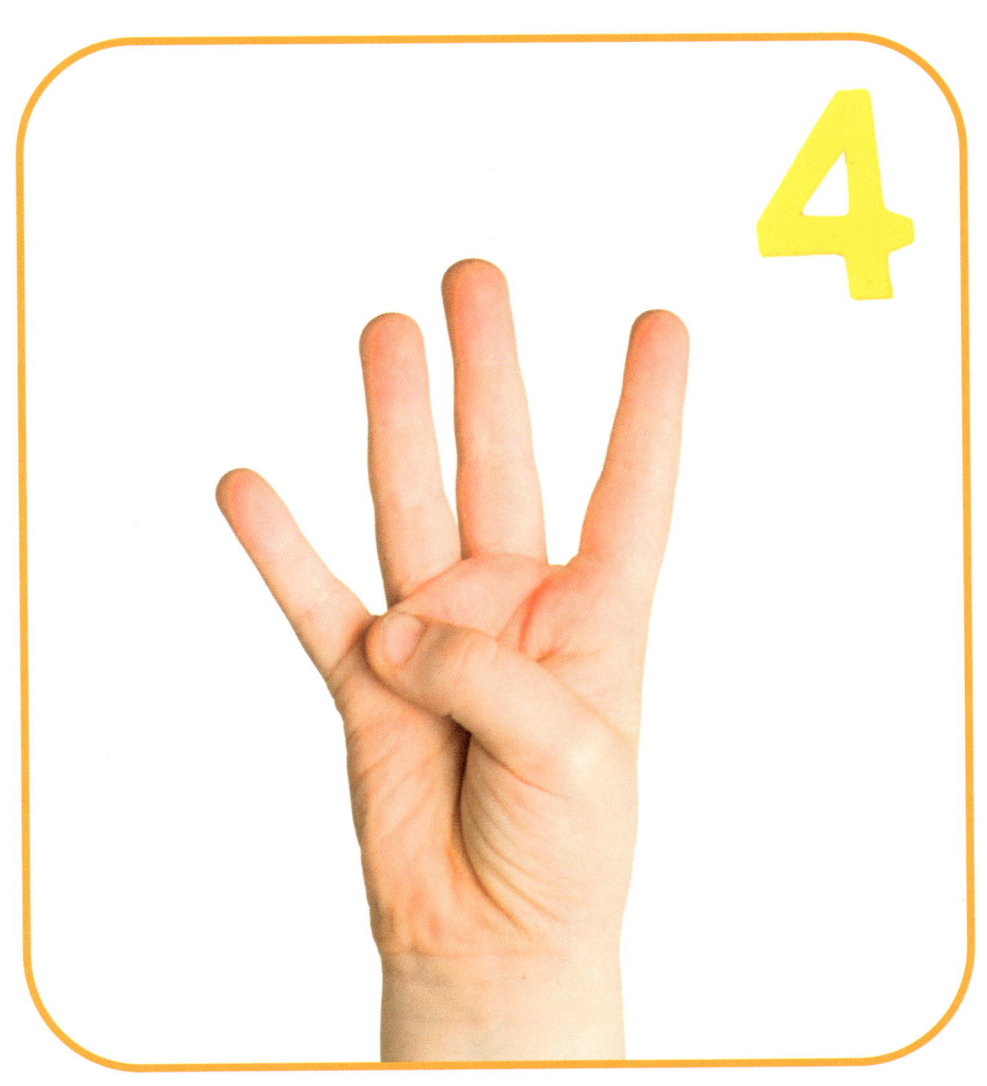

four

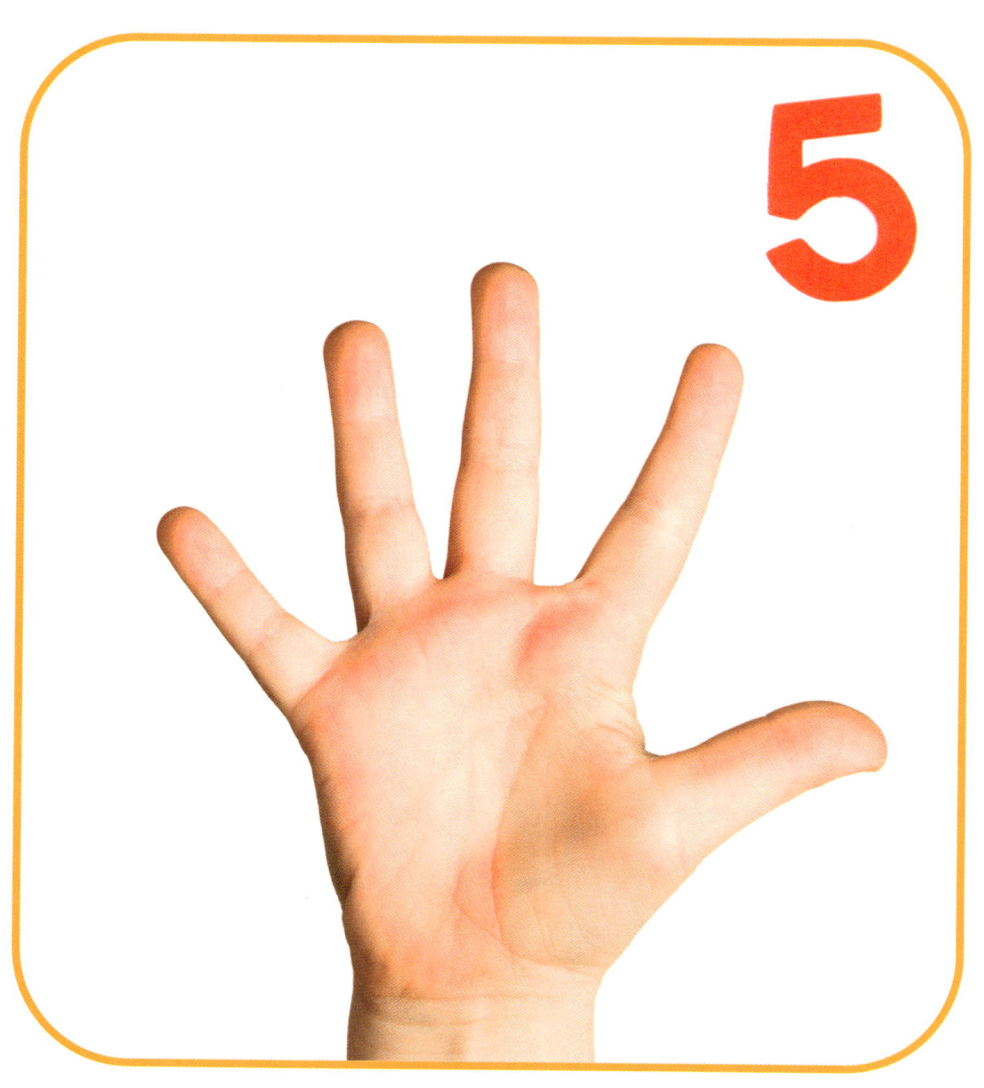

five

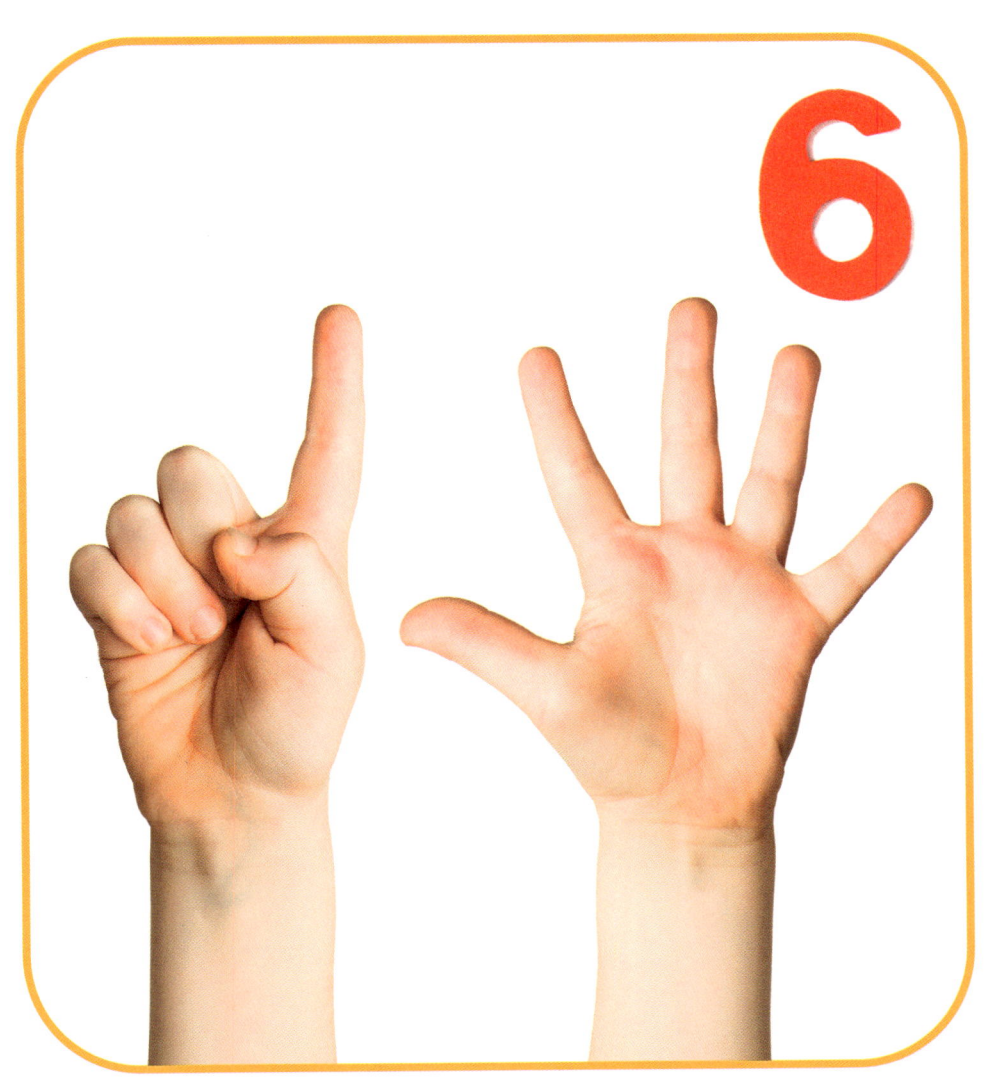

six

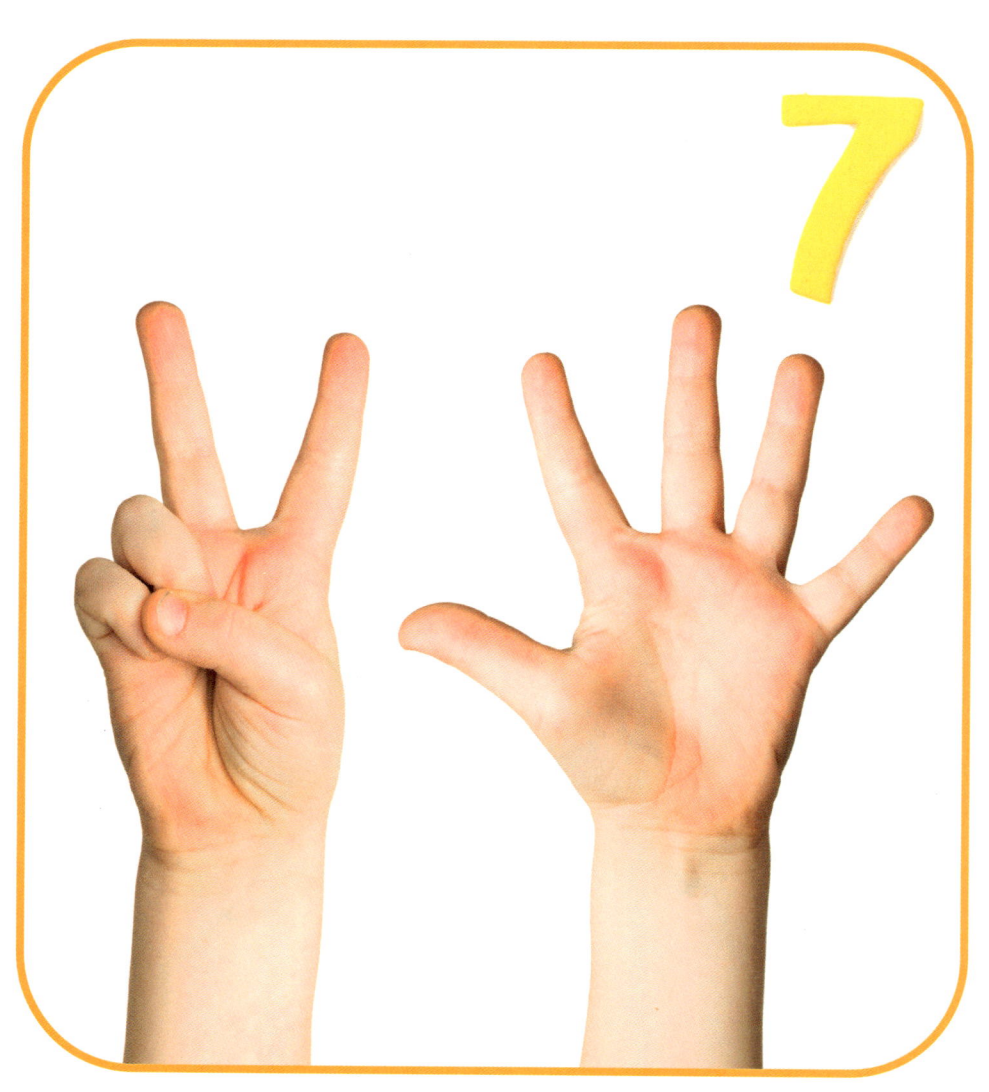

seven

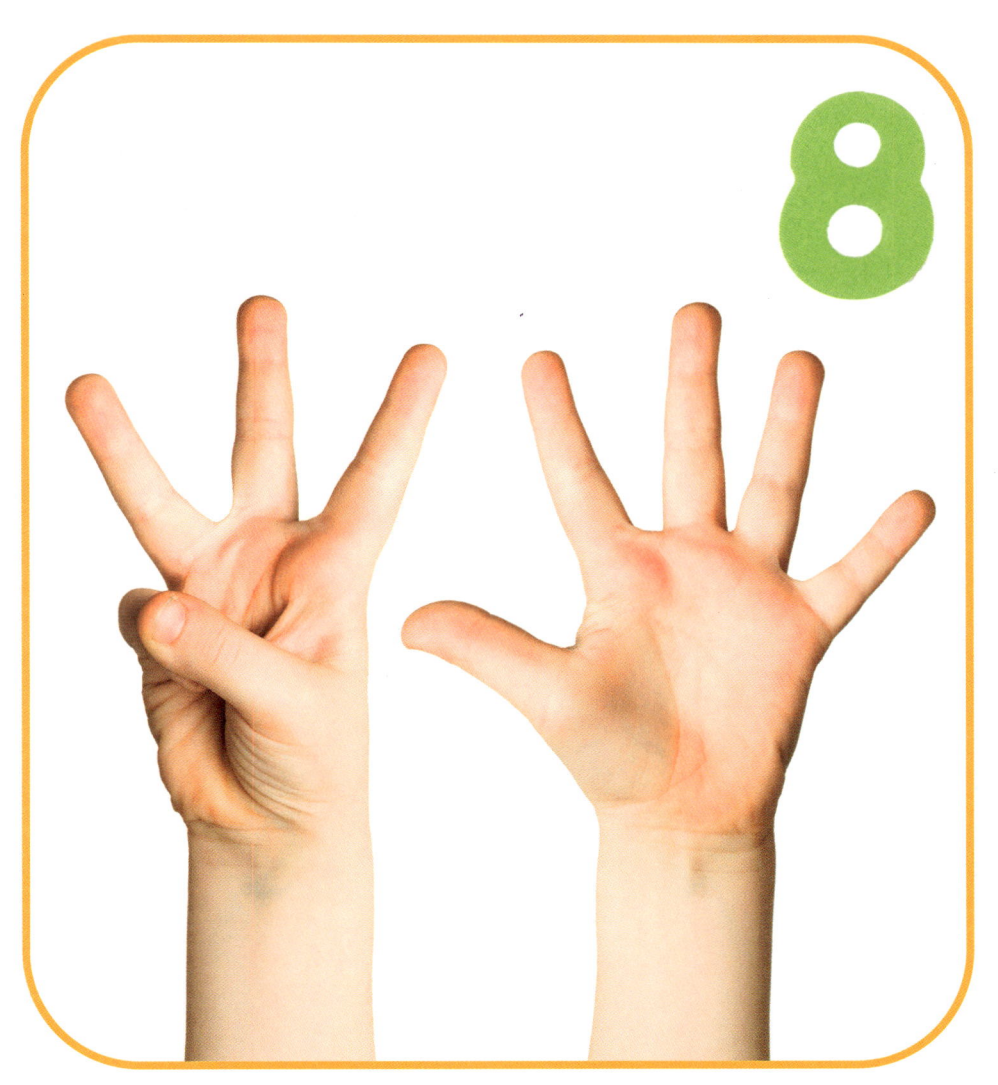

eight

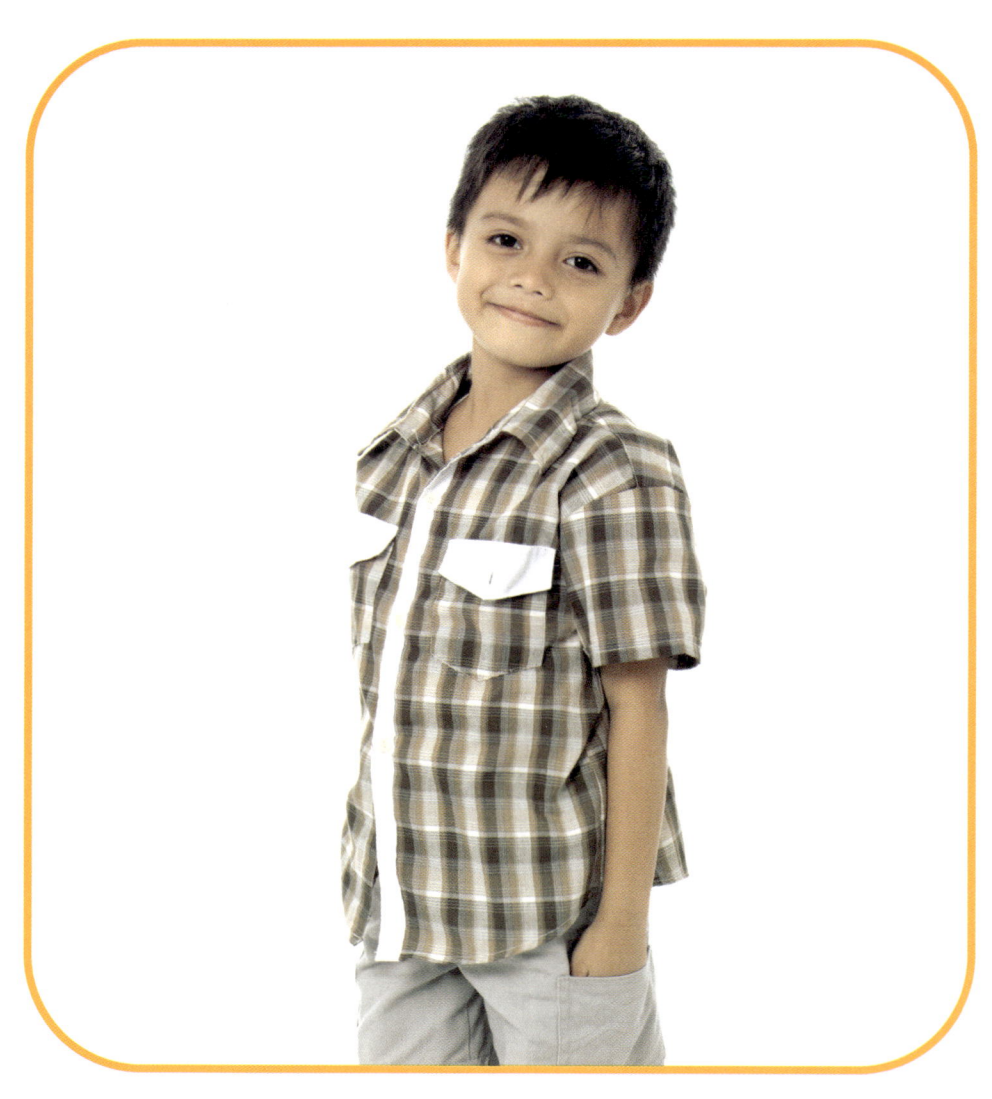

How old are you?

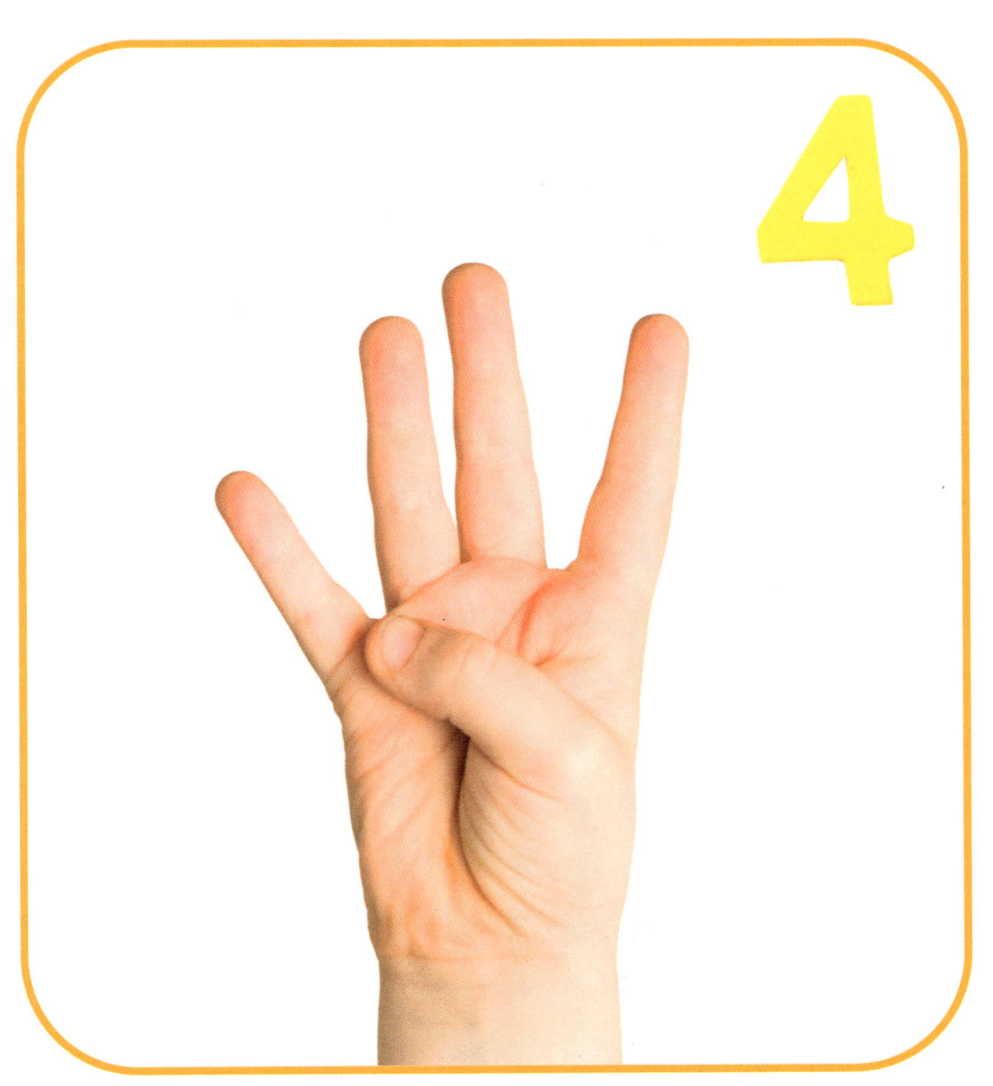

I'm four.

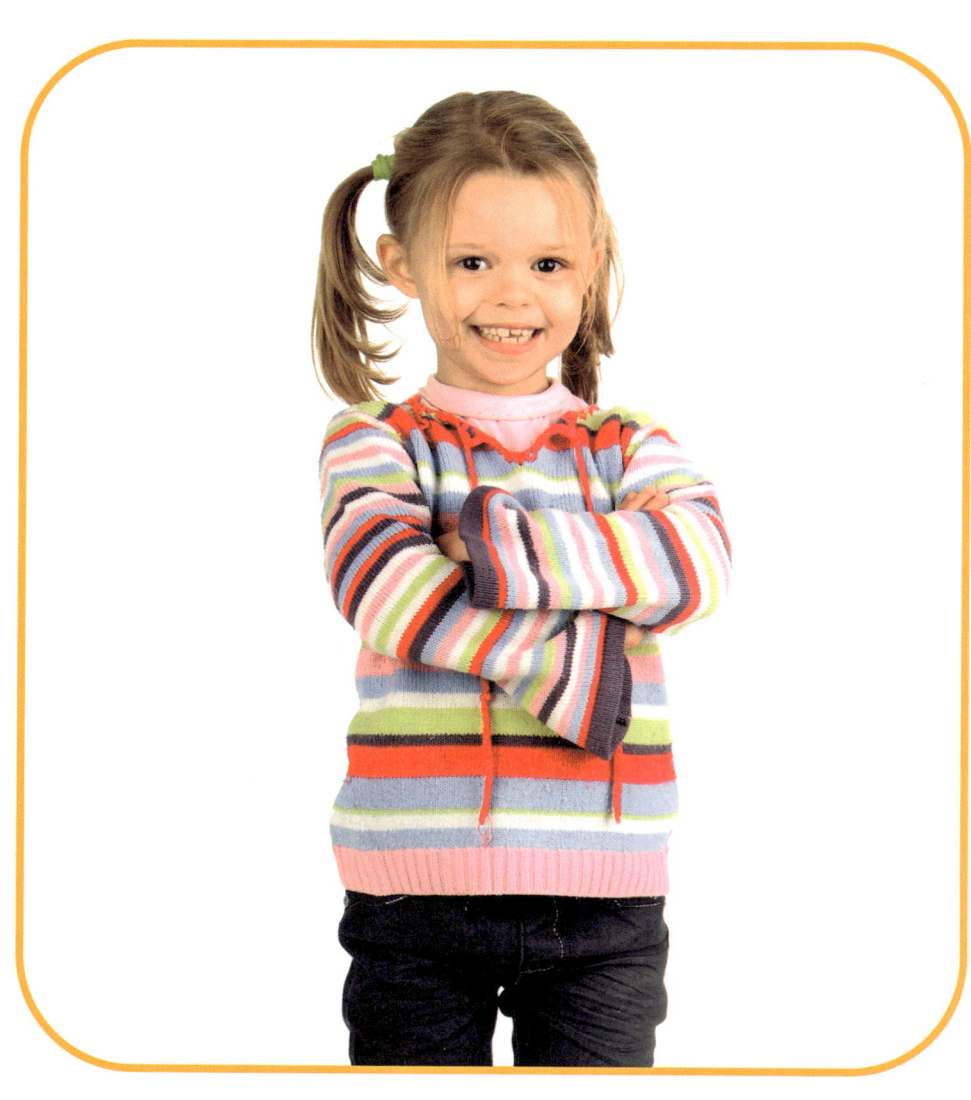

How old are you?

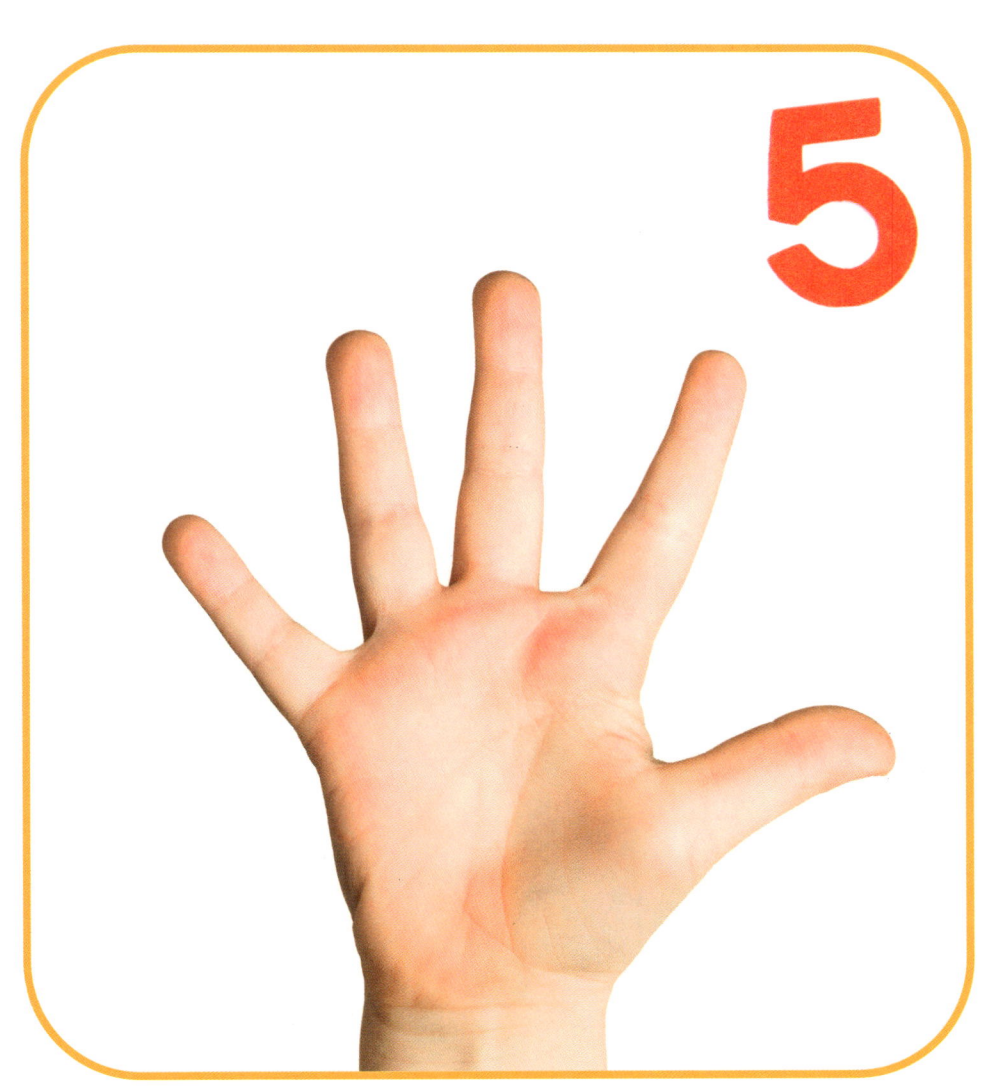

I'm five.

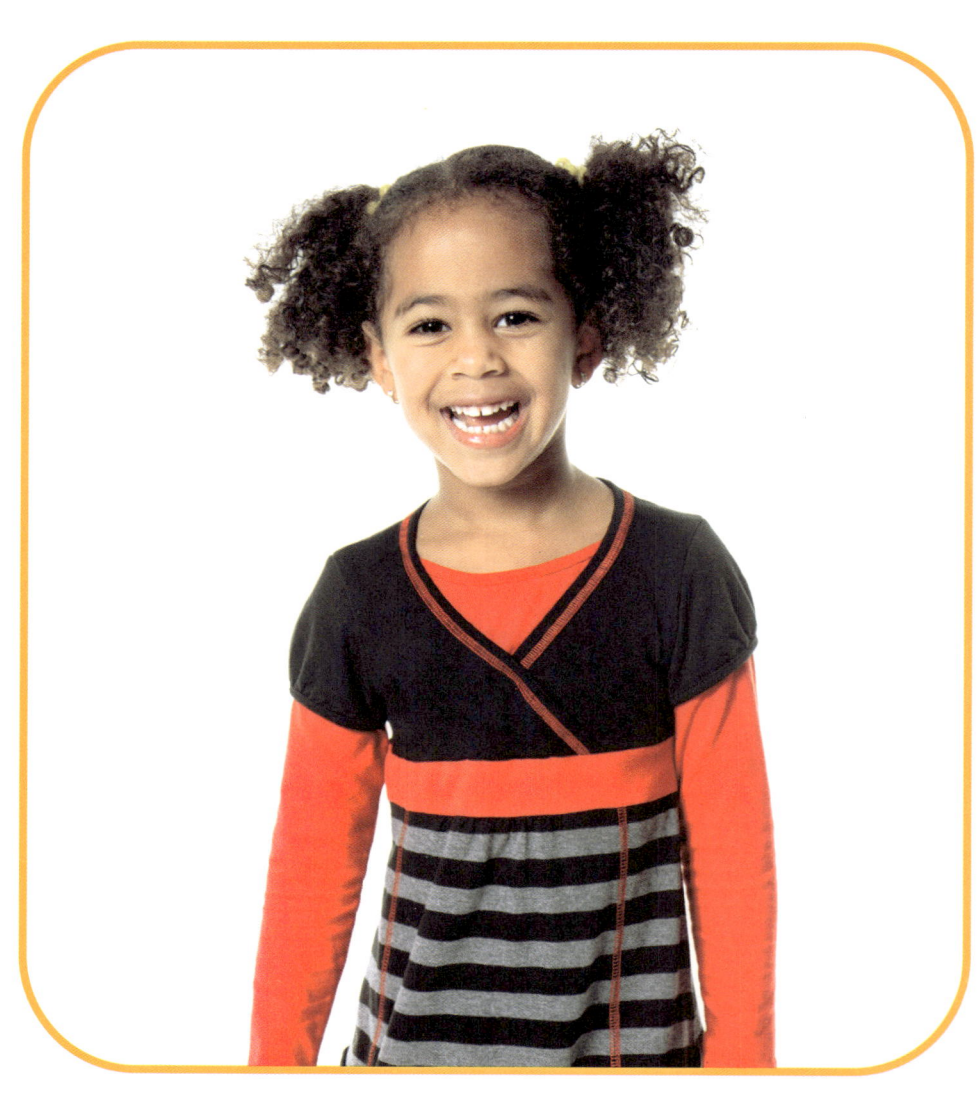

How old are you?

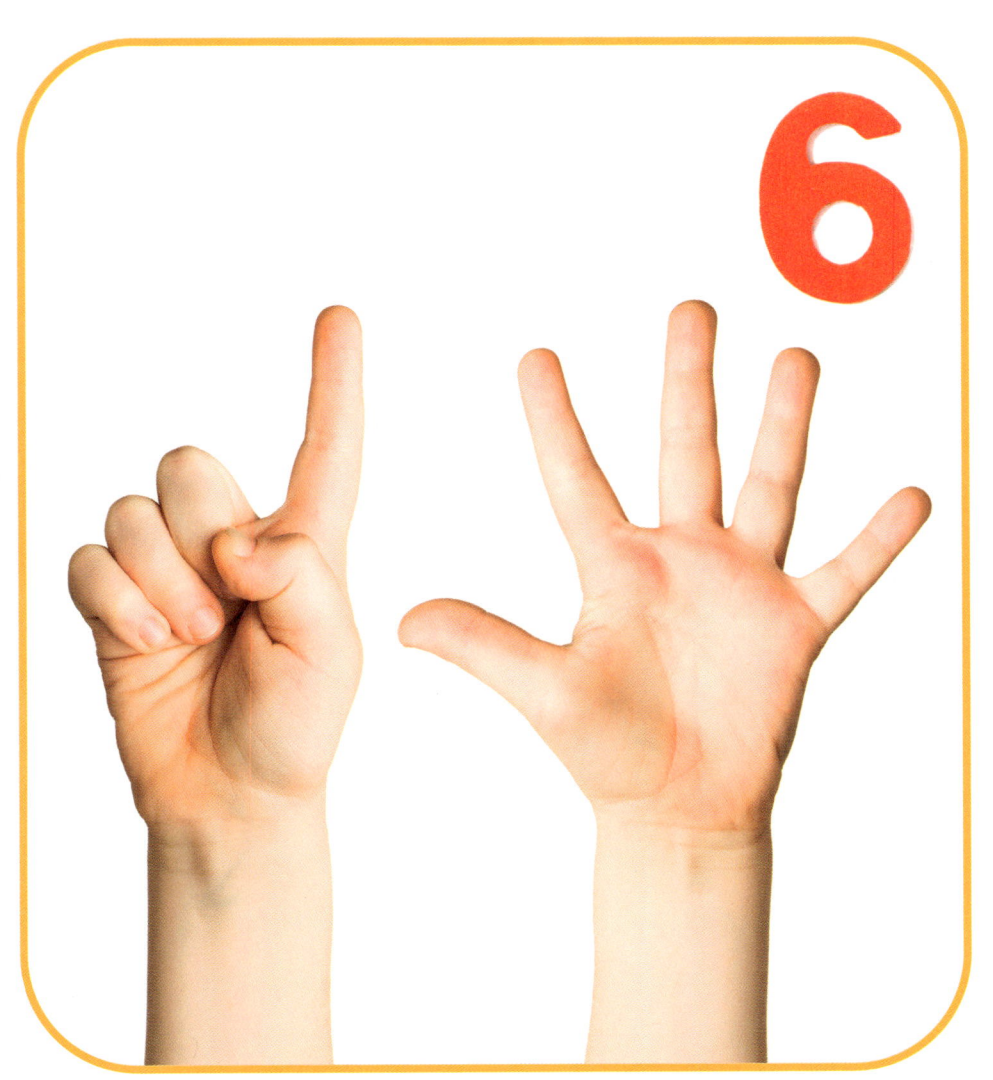

I'm six.

Word List

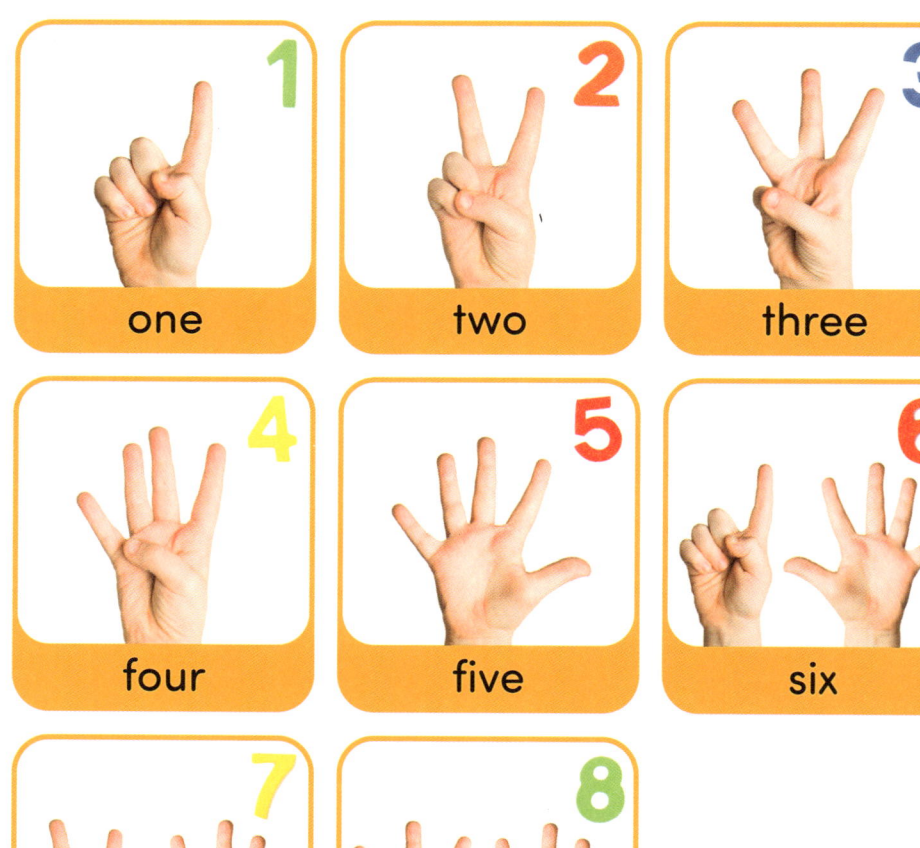

one

two

three

four

five

six

seven

eight